I0132750

Have a
JESUS
FILLED Day

ROY CHAPMAN

Copyright © 2022 by Roy Chapman

All rights reserved. No part of this book may be reproduced or transmitted in any form or by any means, electronic or mechanical, including photocopying, recording, or by any information storage and retrieval system, without permission from the publisher.

Printed in the United States of America. For information, contact:

Jesus Filled Day Publishing Company™

P.O. Box 34

Houston, Texas 77001

WorshipTabernacle.TV

All Scripture quotations, unless otherwise indicated, are taken from the King James Version®. Copyright © 1982 by Thomas Nelson, Inc. Used by permission.

ISBN 978-0-9987486-7-2

TRIBUTE

Ann Chapman's life and ministry was and continues to be a blessing to the Body of Christ. Her contributions to this book project are many and I am thankful for her commitment and dedication. It was an honor to be married to her for 46 years. She is missed by all the people she touched and inspired. Now, she is with her Lord and Savior, Jesus Christ and is deeply missed.

DEDICATION

I dedicate this book to my children and each of their families who are deeply loved and cherished as special gifts from God. My prayer for each of you is that you will allow Jesus to fill each day of your life with His presence.

ACKNOWLEDGMENTS

First and foremost, I give thanks to our Lord Jesus Christ for choosing and trusting me to be His messenger. Jesus, thank you for filling my life with Your precious Holy Spirit each day.

To co-laborers in the ministry, Deborah and Randy Elum, I thank you for encouraging, supporting, praying for, believing in, and, most of all, loving me. Thank you Deborah for your many unique contributions to this book. Your insightful vision inspired me to remain persistent in completing this project.

To Tracie Spradlin, I acknowledge you for your assistance and help with this project. Your faithful love, prayers, and encouragement will always be important to me.

To Brock Beesley, my friend, thank you for the finishing touches you prayerfully added to this book.

To Nancy and Bryan Clement, my special friends, I am honored that you are part of the ministry. Thank you for prayers, encouragement, and love.

To all of the intercessors and prayer warriors in this ministry, who are faithful in your love and service, I give thanks to you. Without your prayers and support I could not fulfill the calling God has given to me. Because you love Him, may He give you a long, healthy, satisfied life, and may all of your days be "Jesus Filled."

To my wife, Judy Chapman, my special friends, Jana and the late Rev. Larry Hinson, Rev. Joe and Pauline Moles, and Linda and the late Rev. Larry Joe Wright, you are all very important to me. I am especially grateful to one of my dearest friends, the late Kenny Hinson, who encouraged me to answer the call of God on my life.

And to many others whose paths I have been fortunate to cross throughout the years, my deepest gratitude, the list would be endless. Everyone is known by the Lord and shall receive their reward from Him (Luke 6:23).

CONTENTS

INTRODUCTION

There was a time when I was not living for God and did not know His promises or His will for my life. Those days were filled with confusion. I missed out on the joys of knowing God. It was a time when I failed to see all the benefits of a life filled with a relationship with the Lord Jesus Christ.

When I rededicated my life to Jesus, I began to study the Word of God and grow spiritually. I learned it is the will of God to heal as well as to save. I learned that it is the will of God to bless His people in their finances.

I learned to walk in the fruit of the Holy Spirit. I learned how to allow my life to be set apart from the things of the world and to serve Jesus in every capacity. My spiritual muscles grew stronger in the years to come as we faced life and death situations in our immediate family. My faith increased in each circumstance and I received miracles in each instance.

In every crisis, I held on to my faith in Jesus Christ. It was important for me to see my family live and not die. When so many of my family members were close to death, I began to take note of the things that really mattered. I began to count my blessings.

The Lord spoke to me these life-changing words,

Have a Jesus Filled Day. Those words became a breath of fresh air and became alive in my spirit. That simple, yet profound truth changed the way I thought about and responded to life to my wife, family, business, relationships, finances, and even Jesus Christ. The Holy Spirit revealed Jesus to me in a new light. No matter what situations or circumstances were going on in my life, He was there to fill my day. I began to see the hand of God and the very atmosphere of Heaven operating in my life. It was the beginning of something wonderful, exciting, and glorious.

I began to be thankful for the small things in life, like driving my youngest daughter to junior high school. As we traveled down the road to her school, I would find out what concerned her. I would talk to her about letting Jesus fill her day.

Sometimes, while I was driving, I would tell her to look at the trees worshipping Jesus and say, "They are letting Him fill up their day." In the spring, as nature blossomed around us, I would say, "Look how the grass and flowers are reaching towards the sun to praise the Lord." Or sometimes, I would share how I had asked Jesus to fill my day with guidance or help me in my work.

The last thing I would tell her before she got out of the car was to *Have a Jesus Filled Day.* I began to find ways to share Jesus with her and teach her how to allow Jesus fill her day, every day.

Words seem inadequate to describe how my

life has been touched and transformed by the principles discussed in this book. The Bible tells us in Acts 10:34 that Jesus is no respecter of persons. What Jesus did for me can be done for all those who believe and let Jesus fill their day.

Read these pages believing that the greatest chapter in your life is about to begin! It is impossible in your own strength. Only as you invite the Holy Spirit to give you a Jesus Filled Day can it happen.

life has become loud and . . . drowned by the gentle
. . . answer . . . to . . . from "the Bible, [the] . . . to
. . . God. It tell you it is now . . . peace and peace
. . . which . . . you for the end . . . beyond . . . and . . . to
. . . but I love . . . and . . . a wonderful . . .

. . . as . . . a . . . peace . . . the . . . to . . . find . . . peace in
. . . chaos in your life is difficult . . . begin . . . to know
. . . step . . . on . . . length . . . in your life . . . when . . .
. . . may . . . the . . . and . . . looking . . . p . . . in . . . of
. . . joy . . .

CHAPTER ONE

A DAY
FILLED WITH
JESUS

". . . 'Sir,' they said, 'we would like to see Jesus.'"
—JOHN 12:21 (NIV)

In John 12:21 we find a specific request from
a group of Greek individuals who had traveled to
Jerusalem for a religious feast. Those Greeks had
heard of Jesus but were not sure whether or not
they could have any
personal connection
with Him. When
they found Jesus' dis-
ciples, their request
was simple. They
told Philip that they
wanted to see Jesus.

> ". . . Sir, we wish to see
> Jesus."
> —JOHN 12:21 (ESV)

Just as personal acquaintance was possible for the
Greeks who desired to see Jesus, it is possible for
you today. He is accessible. Imagine, for a moment,

having Jesus with you all day, every day. That type of connection would change your life and your destiny.

Have you ever thought about spending the day with Jesus? When you think about spending a day with family, whether a mother, a father, children, brothers, sisters, or other relatives, you generally anticipate having a good time. You become excited at the thought of spending a day with close friends, co-workers, or other special individuals.

Most of the time spent with family and friends is predictable. We usually know how they will act, what they will say, and what they will do. Some might be loud while some might be quiet. Some will be the center of attention while others will sit back and observe. Some will be funny while others will be more serious.

But what would it be like to spend a day with Jesus? In the Bible, people responded in many different ways to spending time with Jesus. Martha spent hours in the kitchen preparing for Him when He came. Matthew had Jesus come and eat supper with all of his friends. Zacchaeus, a tax collector, made a commitment to repay everyone he had cheated. Also, groups of 4,000 and 5,000 people forgot about food to hear what Jesus had to say.

But what would it be like for you to spend a day with Jesus? If you were to spend a day with Jesus, what would your conversation be? What would you say? How would you act? What would you want to learn from Him? How would you get to know Him? What would you tell Him about yourself? What would you expect Him to do? What would He say? What would you want to experience with Him?

A Day Filled with Jesus has many benefits. There is abundant life with blessings, victory, miracles, favor, satisfaction, peace, joy, acceptance, forgiveness, guidance, prosperity, protection, and much more!

Why should you seek to have a daily relationship with Jesus? Why should you want to Have a Jesus Filled Day? What difference would it make? Why should you want to ask Him to fill your day with His presence?

> "You make known to me the path of life; you will fill me with joy in your presence, with eternal pleasures at your right hand."
> —PSALM 16:11 (NIV)

There is a dramatic difference between a casual relationship with Jesus and choosing to live for Him on a daily basis. So often in a casual relationship with Jesus, things that this world offer can consume your thoughts, leading to destruction. God does not want you to put other things on a

> "'You shall have no other gods before Me.'"
> —DEUTERONOMY 5:7

higher priority level than your relationship with Him.

In Bible times, people would make idols of wood, metal, or other materials of the day. Those idols had no life of their own. They were the creation of a man. Sadly, people that claimed to serve God would often forsake their relationship with Him to worship an idol made from human hands.

It is easy to imagine that scenario and laugh. It seems almost unbelievable that someone would worship a block of wood instead of a God who performed miraculous sign after miraculous sign. Yet, that is what God's people did on a frequent basis.

The humor fades, however, when you realize that people do similar things today. Some might not bow down to a wooden idol on their kitchen counter, but they let other things in their life become something that they value more than their relationship with Jesus. In our world, things such as television, movies, music, certain individuals, recreation, sports, and other activities can crowd out a relationship with Jesus. While none of those things are wrong, they can easily take a higher priority than a relationship with Christ. It is very important that you let nothing become an "idol" in your life. Many people are searching for satisfaction in life, and some will go to great extremes to achieve it. When you get your heart set on the things of the world and do not have a relationship with Jesus, disaster can overtake you.

That is what happened to one of my sons. He filled his day with the wrong type of friends and a lifestyle which led him to completely forget the Biblical teachings he had received before leaving home. Over a period of ten years, without Jesus in his life, he became addicted to drugs and alcohol. That lifestyle caused destruction in his marriage and the relationship with his children. Things continued to spiral downward until he ended up sleeping in his truck and sometimes under a bridge.

As a parent, I never gave up on him. I continued to pray and believe he would tire of that lifestyle and give his life to Jesus. Eventually, he agreed to enter a Christian rehabilitation program. The principles he learned in rehab worked for a while after he returned home, but he still tried to hang on to his past desires. When he finally realized that true happiness and fulfillment comes from Jesus, he accepted the Lord as his personal Savior. My son's relationship with his children has been restored. He also owns his own home and fills each day with Jesus. That is just one example of what a difference you can experience when you live *A Day Filled with Jesus.*

PEOPLE NEED JESUS

One of the meanings of the name "Jesus" is Savior. He is the true light. When you walk with Him, your path is enlightened so you can see how you should live. We, as humans, have a limited amount of knowledge. No matter how much people learn and study, no one can ever come close to the infinite supply of knowledge that God Almighty possesses. No matter how many years of life experience one has accumulated, it cannot compare to the understanding that God created time, this world, and everything in it. People need our Creator. People need Jesus.

> "Your word is a lamp to my feet and a light to my path."
> —PSALM 119:105 (ESV)

In John 14:6 Jesus told the people that He alone was the Way, the Truth, and the Life. He was the One who said that no person can come to God, the Father, except by Him.

In Romans 10:9 (NIV) the Word says, "That if you confess with your mouth, 'Jesus is Lord', and believe in your heart that God raised Him from the dead, you will be saved." If you accept Jesus as your Savior, you can have A Day Filled with Jesus every day of your life.

> "That if thou confess with thy mouth the Lord Jesus, and shalt believe in thine heart that God hath raised Him from the dead, thou shalt be saved."
> —ROMANS 10:9

God has incredible creative power. Think about that for a minute. God created everything in the world from nothing (Genesis 1:1). By His power He was able to transform a world that was "without form" and "void" into the beautiful planet that we live on today. God also has the power to take a nobody and turn them into a somebody. As you turn through the pages of the Bible, you find story after story of men and women that had real problems. They had real issues. And yet, the power of God was able to change them and their circumstances. Jesus can make something out of your nothing. He is the Creator.

Many brand new vehicles today come with a warranty. Imagine having a problem with your vehicle. Instead of taking it to the proper service department of the dealership where you purchased it, you take it to another garage without the right tools to have it fixed. That doesn't make any sense, does it? However, we do that very thing with our own lives. We go anywhere and everywhere asking people how to fix our lives instead of going to our Creator.

People have a tendency to tell their sad stories to each other as if one more heart wrenching tale will help them in some way. Some people talk so much about the medication they take, you would get the impression they are proud that they constantly visit the doctor's office to obtain another prescription. There's nothing wrong with doctors or medicine. However, when people think that medication is the only thing they need, that is all they have to talk about. If people would talk about the Creator, they could assure others that the only thing they need is Jesus. They could tell people to take whatever ails them, or whatever malfunction they have, back to the manufacturer; the One who created them. They could assure others that they are still under warranty. Jesus will fix their life. If you

> "Nay, in all these things we are more than conquerors through him who loved us."
>
> —ROMANS 8:37

know Jesus, be bold to spread the news. Just like the vehicle covered by the service contract, you are covered and should stand and say, "I'm under warranty. I'm under the Word of God."

What do people need? *Jesus.* If you have Jesus, you can have confidence in knowing that you are more than a conqueror. "For I am convinced that neither death nor life, neither angels nor demons, neither the present nor the future, nor any powers, neither height nor depth, nor anything else in all creation, will be able to separate us from the love of God that is in Christ Jesus our Lord," (Romans 8:38-39 NIV). Keep His commandments; He is a strong tower, a sure foundation. There will be safety in your walk, and you will not stumble in darkness. If you are spending your day with Jesus, He will hold your hand so you will not stumble when trials and tribulations come. In your daily walk, pursue Jesus. Seek Him and you will find Him.

A DAY
FILLED WITH
JESUS

DAILY CONFESSION

Thank You, Lord, that as I desire to meet with You today, You desire to meet me in return. Thank You that I recognize my need for You. I don't need anyone or anything other than You. As I seek You, I will find You, according to Your Word.

Today, *I have A Day Filled with Jesus!*

CHAPTER TWO

A DAY
FILLED WITH
LIFE

"Death and life are in the power of the tongue:
and they that love it shall eat the fruit thereof."
—PROVERBS 18:21

The Word of God says that you will receive what
you say. If you want life, not death and destruction,
you must speak to your problems. Then, believe in
your heart, and watch the problems disappear. There is power in the words of prayer and speech. Negative speaking comes from wrong thinking and closes the door to faith in God and His grace.

> "Death and life are in
> the power of the tongue:
> and they that love it
> shall eat the fruit there-
> of."
> —PROVERBS 18:21

The power of God comes from His revealed will in His Word, the Bible. As a Christian, you need to renew your mind daily (Romans 12:1-21). You must choose to think on things that are true, things that are noble, things that are just, things that are pure, things that are lovely, and things that are of good report (Philippians 4:8). Understand that you are not ruled by circumstances. The words that come out of your mouth are a reflection of what you are thinking. They are a reflection of what you are feeling. And most importantly, they are a reflection of what you truly believe. The Bible tells us in Proverbs that as we think in our mind and heart, so we speak.

Late one night, I was rocking my youngest daughter, as I did most every night, but something was different about that night. In the midst of rocking her, I asked my wife, to dial 911. As I handed my daughter to her, fear filled my eyes. I had been complaining of chest pains, and when I called my wife, she sensed that I was having a heart attack.

"Finally, brethren, whatsoever things are true, whatsoever things are honest, whatsoever things are just, whatsoever things are pure, whatsoever things are lovely, whatsoever things are of good report; if there be any virtue, and if there be any praise, think on these things."
—PHILIPPIANS 4:8

She immediately called an ambulance. When the paramedics arrived, they would not let my wife ride in the ambulance with me to the hospital. As she followed in her car, she told me later that she was appreciative for the opportunity to have some time alone with God. That time with God allowed her trust and faith in His Word to increase. She arrived at the hospital with full confidence in God that if I was having a heart attack, I would not die but live to continue serving the Lord and declaring the works of God.

Several years earlier, when my mother-in-law died of breast cancer, my wife said that she had been "destroyed for lack of knowledge" (Hosea 4:6). That verse applied to both of us because we did not know how to call out to God for help to see her healed. We had not learned the Scriptures that teach us how to pray for the sick. We didn't know that it was God's will to heal just as it was His will to save.

But on this occasion, as I was in the ambulance and she was following behind in my car, she felt as if Jesus was sitting beside her as she

> "My people are destroyed from lack of knowledge..."
> —HOSEA 4:6 (NIV)

spoke life to my heart and claimed healing and restoration for my body. In the emergency room, I was quickly hooked up to monitors and several doctors were called in. My wife overheard one doctor tell me that I had damage to the back of my heart. That really concerned her, so I told her to tell the children that I loved them. I did not believe that I would live to tell them again myself. Personally, my wife was convinced that I would be all right. Her greatest concern was to break the spirit of fear and death and convince me that I would live.

About that time, another ambulance brought in some injured people who had been in a severe car accident. One of them was placed in the bed next to me, and they began talking about someone involved in the accident who had been killed. Hearing someone talk about death seemed to make me more fearful. My mother died of a heart attack at the age of forty and my father had a major heart attack at an early age. That was my first life and death situation since I recommitted my life to the Lord. The doctors did three days of testing on me. During that time, I stood in faith, trusting that the Lord was healing my heart. At the conclusion of those three days, no trace of damage to my heart was found. Jesus had spared my life and miraculously repaired my heart. That truly was *A Day Filled with Life!*

Looking back, I realize that the situation with my heart was a test of my faith. In years that followed, there were major challenges as my faith continued to be put to the test. Several of my children and I have faced life and death situations. Giving glory to God, I am happy to say that in each circumstance I chose to speak life to the situation and have a testimony of the miraculous power of God for each incident.

To have A Day Filled with Life, you must put Jesus first in your heart and mind. Jesus is life and the giver of life. Yes, you can exist without Him, but you will not have the fullness of joy and peace He promises in His Word unless, you make Him the center of your life. The Bible says that Jesus came to give us life. The life that He gives is not just an ordinary life, but an abundant life blessed with joy, peace, love, prosperity, and good health.

> "Beloved, I pray that you may prosper in all things and be in health, just as your soul prospers."
> —3 JOHN 1:2 (NAS)

My oldest daughter makes a wonderful spaghetti sauce. The sauce involves numerous ingredients, including many different spices, herbs, vegetables, and other condiments. It is *possible* to make her spaghetti sauce without all of the ingredients, but it wouldn't taste anything like it is meant to taste. It would taste bland and dull, lacking the benefits of its full potential if all the ingredients were not added to the sauce.

In the same way, it is God's desire for each of us to be complete. Second Timothy 3:16-17 states it this way, "All scripture is given by inspiration of

God, and is profitable for doctrine, for reproof, for correction, for instruction in righteousness: That the man of God may be perfect, thoroughly furnished unto all good works." God wants us to be sound in our body, sound in our faith, and sound in our mind. Each day He places before us blessings or curses. He tells us to choose life, and that is what we pray you will speak today. Let each day of your life be filled with Jesus.

YOUR TALK BECOMES YOUR ACTIONS

Are you thinking the way Christ thinks, or are you thinking the way the world thinks? Do you know that Christ does not think the way the world thinks? If you are going to have A Day Filled with Life, you are going to have to change your thinking. You need to renew your mind and start thinking correctly. Jesus wants you to change the way you think, the things you say, and even the things you do. Jesus wants you to have His mind. Your thoughts will be totally different once you start meditating and thinking on the Word of God. Proverbs 23:7 says that as a man thinks in his heart, so is he. That means that whatever you think will eventually become an action.

" . . . I have set before you life and death, blessing and cursing: therefore choose life, that both thou and thy seed may live."
—Deuteronomy 30:19

As followers of Jesus Christ, it is very important to know that we all have the ability to control our thoughts. The state of a person depends on who, or what, controls their mind. According to Romans 8:6-7, "For to be carnally minded is death; but to be spiritually minded is life and peace. Because the carnal mind is enmity against God: for it is not subject to the law of God, neither indeed can be." If people are going to participate in the things of God, they have to cast their flesh to the side and start to do the things of the Spirit. In other words, subdue the flesh and allow the Holy Spirit to teach you how to become a "doer" of the Word of God.

In the Old Testament, Moses' day was so full of God that when he came down from Mount Sinai, where he had encountered the Living God, the Bible says that his face glowed with the glory of God. Moses was unaware of God's glorious presence in him and on him. Everyone that saw him knew that he had been with God. That type of experience was not just available for Moses. It exists for everyone today. Whether you are with

> "It came about when Moses was coming down from Mount Sinai (and the two tablets of the testimony were in Moses' hand as he was coming down from the mountain), that Moses did not know that the skin of his face shone because of his speaking with Him."
> —EXODUS 34:29

31

God in His presence to worship Him, or He is working and living His presence through you, life will be different.

FIRST THINGS FIRST

When Jesus fills your day with His life, you will begin to think different, act different, and even talk different. You will change as more of His mind moves in and more of your thoughts, opinions, and character move out. In Matthew 6:33, Jesus said, "But seek first the kingdom of God, and His righteousness . . ." When you put Jesus first in your daily thinking and activities, you can truly begin to have *A Day Filled with Life*.

Life will change. Schedules will change. The way you used to deal with anxieties and hurts that would control your emotions and actions will change. You will have new choices and options as you enter into a life filled with an abundance of blessings.

Have a
JESUS
Filled Day

A DAY
FILLED WITH
LIFE

DAILY CONFESSION

Thank You, Lord, that there is power in Your Word. Thank You that as I speak Your Word, in faith, I am able to have confidence that You will answer every prayer that I pray. Thank You that I am delivered from all death and destruction. Thank You that my life has been redeemed from the pit of death and despair. I believe that as I confess Your Word, I receive everything that I pray, in the name of Jesus.

Today, *I have A Day Filled with Life!*

CHAPTER THREE

A DAY
FILLED WITH
BLESSINGS

"Blessed shall you be in the city, and blessed
shall you be in the country."
—DEUTERONOMY 28:3 (NAS)

Ann and I had been living in our new home
in the country for a few months but she appeared
frustrated and sad. I could tell that she was still feeling overwhelmed and stressed about living there.
We had lived in the same house for over twenty
five years and the building of our new home had
continued to weigh her down.

Building our new home had been planned
for quite some time. We had been saving money
since we had been married. We often worked two
jobs, believing one day we would sell the house we
raised our five children in and build a nice home
in the country. Our new home was twice the size of
our other house and I began to think we had made

a mistake building such a large home. After all, four of our five children were married and we only had one child left at home.

SATAN'S GOAL IS TO KEEP YOU DISTRACTED

Other frustrations began to surface. It was only a five-minute drive to work from our old house. However, from our new home in the country my wife had to drive almost an hour to get to the office, fighting heavy traffic. Each day, it seemed, she resented it and could not see the blessing God had given us with our new home. Those situations might seem small to you, but they were significant to her at the time. They were big issues to her because Satan tried to focus her attention on petty and negative thoughts. He tried to make her forget the blessings God had given to us.

She told me that one morning around 3:00 am, she was returning to our bedroom from the kitchen after getting a glass of water. As she came through the family room she looked out of the large windows. She paused when she noticed the moon shining brightly through the tall pine trees in the backyard. Suddenly, the Lord spoke to her, and for the first time since we had moved into our new home, she realized how very blessed we were.

There she was, a little farm girl from rural Arkansas who did not have electricity until the age of eight. Neither did she have running water or inside plumbing. God had blessed her so much and had brought her so far. She thanked the Lord Jesus for revealing to her, that night, the tremendous blessing that she experienced in the form of her new home.

She said, "Lord, how beautiful this home is," as she looked around the room.

"Forgive me for overlooking the blessings you have bestowed upon our family. You have given us this beautiful new home in the country with windows throughout the back of the house, and lights shining everywhere."

That night, she felt God reassure her that we had not made a mistake in building such a large home. Our home was blessed with peace and serenity. In the years that have followed, we were able to use our home to bless many visiting ministers and evangelists. In the end, she realized that she had no reason to be stressed. She had no

> "You will be blessed in the city and blessed in the country."
> —DEUTERONOMY 28:3 (NIV)

reason to be frustrated because she was experiencing A Day Filled with Blessings.

As you read this book, you may not have a new home in the country. You do not have to have a new home in the country or the city to be blessed each day. The Bible tells us that all are blessed when they have a relationship with Jesus Christ. Galatians 3:13-14 tells us that, "Christ has redeemed us so that the blessing of Abraham might come upon the Gentiles in Christ Jesus, that we might receive the promise of the Spirit through faith." As you read that Scripture you might be wondering, "What is a Gentile?" From a Biblical understanding, a Gentile refers to every person that does not have a Jewish heritage.

That Scripture is telling you and me that every single person on the face of the earth has the potential to have the blessing of God on their life. Originally, it was reserved for God's chosen people who trace their roots to Abraham. The sacrifice of Jesus Christ on the cross is the reason all humanity can receive that same blessing. If you have a relationship with Him, you can be sure that your Jesus Filled Day includes A Day Filled with Blessings! Everything you put your hands to is blessed. Be thankful for what He has given to you and bless His name each day.

> "Christ redeemed us . . ."
> —GALATIANS 3:13
> (NIV)

WAVES UPON WAVES OF BLESSINGS

Have you ever watched the waves in an ocean? One wave will come and then another will come in on the heels of the first wave. God operates in the same way. He will bestow blessing after blessing like the waves in an ocean. Have you ever tried to write down all the blessings of the Lord that belong to you? He wants to bless you beyond your wildest imagination; so much so, that everybody around you will be blessed because of you. You can see this in the life of Jacob (Genesis

30:27). While he worked for his Uncle Laban, Laban's entire house experienced the blessing of God because Jacob was blessed.

Almost everybody in the world believes in Heaven. We have read or heard about how wonderful Heaven will be. However, many people think that living for Jesus doesn't come with any blessings here on earth. They fail to realize that "Every good gift and every perfect gift is from above . . ." (James 1:17). God has a multitude of blessings that are available to you today that far outweigh any benefits this world claims to offer.

Your Heavenly Father owns everything; even the cattle on a thousand hills belong to Him. He loves to bestow His blessings upon His children. If you want the abundance that the Lord has for you, declare all the blessings of God over your life. Declare that you are blessed coming and going and everything your hands touch is blessed. Do not miss the blessings that God has for you! He wants to bless your life with success, achievement, and triumph. The Bible is full of promises for everyone to claim; personal well-being, victory over failure and destruction, and so much more.

> "Every good and perfect gift is from above . . ."
> —JAMES 1:17 (NIV)

A DAY
FILLED WITH
BLESSINGS

DAILY CONFESSION

Thank You, Lord, that I am blessed in every way. I am the head and not the tail; above and not beneath. Thank You for every blessing You have brought to my life. I do not take any of them for granted but am grateful that You love me and cause me to be blessed because I love You. I do not operate in fear. I do not operate under stress, but I am open to receive every good and perfect gift that You have for me.

Today, *I have A Day Filled with Blessings!*

A DAY
FILLED WITH
VICTORY

"But thanks be to God, who gives us the victory
through our Lord Jesus Christ."
—1 CORINTHIANS 15:57

Mark 4:35-40 tells a wonderful story of Jesus
and His disciples. Jesus made a decision to go from
one side of a lake to the other. After embarking on
the journey by boat, Jesus laid down to get some
rest.

It wasn't too long after He had fallen asleep
that a storm arose on the water. His disciples were
frantic, worrying for their lives as they attempted
to deal with the storm at hand. Finally, Jesus' disciples woke Him up, frustrated that He was com-
fortable enough to sleep during their crisis.

Jesus amazed them when He responded to their fear by turning to the wind and the sea, saying, ". . . Peace, be still! . . ." (v. 39). Immediately, the wind died down and the water became calm.

> ". . . In the world you shall have tribulation; but be of good cheer, I have overcome the world."
> —JOHN 16:33

Because the disciples had not handled the situation in the same manner He did, Jesus asked them, ". . . Why are you so fearful? How is it that you have no faith?" (v. 40).

YOUR VICTORY IS ON THE OTHER SIDE

In an allegorical sense, Jesus is telling some of you to get in a boat and go to the other side of the lake. Does that mean you will not have any problems? Or mean that you will not encounter storms along the way? No, not at all. The Word of God says that in this world you are going to have tribulations. But be of good cheer, He has promised He will be with you to help you to the other side of your problems. Remember that through your storm, you can see great victory.

REJOICING BRINGS ABOUT VICTORY

There are certain things that are out of your control. You cannot control who your parents are. You cannot control what color your eyes are. You cannot control the country in which you were born. But, you can control how you choose to respond to problems. We all have different ways of responding to problems. You can operate in trust or doubt. You can respond with faith or fear. You can be confident or afraid. You always have the ability to choose your response. So, whether it is a stormy or sunny day in your life, it is still a day that the Lord has made, and you should rejoice and be glad in it (Psalm 118:24). Why? When you rejoice, it brings about change and you can have A Day Filled with Victory.

> "This is the day the Lord has made; let us rejoice and be glad in it."
> —PSALM 118:24 (ESV)

YOUR PROBLEMS ARE NOT BIGGER THAN YOUR GOD

Having a Jesus Filled Day does not mean that you will not have problems. The Word of God tells us that we are all in this world, and that tribulations and heartaches will come (John 8:23, 16:33). You need to remember that your problems are not bigger than the Almighty God.

I do not know what storm is in your life today. It could be sickness, financial problems, family problems, or job-related problems. You need to give your problems to Jesus and leave them with Him. First Peter 5:7 tells you to cast all of your cares on Jesus. That refers to your worries, your anxieties, and your concerns. Leave them with Jesus. Don't try to take them back from Him and deal with them yourself. You will never be able to handle your problems like Jesus can handle your problems. *Victory is never guaranteed when you try to handle problems on your own.* It's only when you have faith in God to deal with the situation that victory is assured. Pray, believe, and stand on His Word to receive the answer. The key to letting Jesus handle your problems is to use the Word of God. Jesus has given you authority over every situation you will encounter, big or small. When you speak the Word of God and operate in the authority that you have as a child of God, you are giving all of your problems to Jesus to handle. You are giving Him permission to take care of the situation. So today, speak to your storm and press on to the other side. Press onto victory.

> "Come near to God and he will come near to you . . ." —JAMES 4:8 (NIV)

In Matthew 9:20-22, there was a woman who, for twelve years, had dealt with severe hemorrhaging. The Bible tells us that she had spent all of her money on doctors and yet her situation had not improved. Somehow she heard that Jesus, the Healer, was coming to her town. She began to make her way through the crowd, determined to press her way to Him. She was tired of living a life of defeat and disease. She knew that day would be her day for victory; the day she would be healed. "And suddenly, a woman who had a flow of blood for twelve years came from behind and touched the hem of His garment. For she said to herself, 'If only I may touch His garment, I shall be made well.' But Jesus turned around, and when He saw her He said, 'Be of good cheer, daughter; your faith has made you well.' And the woman was made well from that hour." She was determined to have a Jesus Filled Day, A Day Filled with Victory.

> "But thanks be to God, Who gives us the victory (as conquerors) through our Lord Jesus Christ."
> —1 CORINTHIANS 15:57 (AMP)

Jesus told you that He is closer than a brother. You don't have to crawl on your hands and knees to come to Him. You can reach out to Jesus, knowing you can touch Him throughout the day. He is near to you and wants to be exactly what you need Him to be.

YOU NEED TO GET IN THE BOAT AND SAIL ON

A few years ago, I was at a lake in Houston. While there, I saw a couple of guys out on the water with a boat. However, they weren't completely in the boat, their feet dangled in the water as they sat on the edge. Eventually, their weight was too great and the boat flipped over, submerging them in the lake. Instead of using the boat properly, which was made to carry them, they chose to play around and eventually the boat turned over on them. Those young men probably felt that they were perfectly safe sitting on the edge. They probably thought that they didn't need to be completely in the boat. Using that scenario as an analogy, when you are not fully in the will of God it can lead to undesirable consequences.

What has Jesus told you to do, but you won't get all the way in the boat? Are you trying to achieve satisfaction by doing things your way, believing that your plan is as safe and secure as the direction that God gives? Get in the boat. Trust in the Lord. He has your best interest in His heart. In the book of Jeremiah God tells us: "'For I know the thoughts that I think toward you,' says the LORD, 'thoughts of peace and not of evil, to give you a future and a hope,'" (Jeremiah 29:11).

> "'For I know the plans I have for you,' declares the Lord, 'plans to prosper you and not to harm you, plans to give you hope and a future."
> —JEREMIAH 29:11 (NIV)

As Christopher Columbus and his crew sailed toward America, all they could see for days was water. In the natural, it looked like they would not find the New World. He was asked, "What do you want us to do?" Although he saw nothing but water, it was recorded in his log that he said these words: "Sail on." Christopher Columbus knew that if he continued to move forward, he would eventually reach his goal. He continued because he believed the New World existed. As long as he persevered and did not give up, he was convinced that he would see victory from his efforts.

You must possess that same perseverance and "sail on." Do not give up in the midst of your journey. The abundance of your blessing is greater than what you had to go through to get there. Do not look at your past circumstances, allowing them to hinder you from going forward. You could be on the verge of a victorious breakthrough.

DO NOT TURN BACK, A FRESH WIND IS ON THE WAY

You will have many opportunities to lose heart and turn back. I want to encourage you not to forget that if you keep going, Jesus will be there with you – through every fire, trial, and tribulation. Do not be moved by what you see, hear, or feel. Instead, stand firm in what you believe. Obstacles will come and try to hinder your progress and slow you down. Do not deviate from what Jesus has told you. The Bible says that weapons will be formed against you, but they will not prosper (Isaiah 54:17).

"No weapon that is formed against you shall prosper . . ."
—ISAIAH 54:17

There was another time when the disciples were in a boat, straining against the wind and the waves. That time, however, Jesus was not with them. They were doing everything in their power to cross the lake but to no avail. Like the disciples, you might feel like you are putting a lot of effort into reaching the other side of the lake. And similar to their situation, it doesn't look like you are getting closer to your destination.

> "Behold, I give unto you power to tread on serpents and scorpions, and over all the power of the enemy: and nothing shall by any means hurt you." —LUKE 10:19

Have faith and trust that God will send a fresh wind your way. He did it for the disciples when Jesus came walking to them on the water that night. The gospel of John, chapter 6, tells us that after Jesus climbed into the boat and the waves died down, they were immediately at the other side of the lake. That's what I call a fresh wind! What once was a wind of defeat became a fresh wind of change and victory.

THERE IS VICTORY IN UNDERSTANDING YOUR AUTHORITY

What are you expecting in life? Are you anticipating good things or bad things? Are you walking and confessing authority over your life, or are you allowing circumstances or feelings to dull your enthusiasm for life? If so, you are imprisoning yourself with a negative frame of mind?

It is important that, as a Christian, you understand the authority you have in Christ Jesus and function in that authority. He has given you power and authority over the very sin that has bound you in the past. Nothing by any means will hurt you. Whatever situation tries to come your way, Christ has given you the power to overcome it.

ACTIVATE YOUR AUTHORITY

You activate your authority by speaking the Word and praying the Word. To activate your authority you have to say it, not just think it. There is a Scripture in Proverbs 18:21 that says, "Death and life are in the power of the tongue . . ." Notice that the Scripture does not say that death and life are in the power of your thoughts. Why not? Because when you speak, you are giving life to your thoughts. There is power in your words. That is why Jesus told the disciples,

> "Truly I tell you, if anyone says to this mountain, 'Go throw yourself into the sea,' and does not doubt in their heart but believes that what they say will happen, it will be done for them."
> —MARK 11:23 (NIV)

". . . if ye shall say to this mountain, 'Be removed and be cast into the sea,' it will shall be done. And whatsoever things, ye shall ask in prayer, believing, ye shall receive," (Matthew 21:21-22). The key is understanding that your authority is released as you speak the Word of God.

It is important that you exercise your authority. Authority is like a weight room full of equipment. You can let it sit unused until it rusts and becomes inoperable. Or, you can use it to develop your muscles to strengthen you because you understand the benefits of using the equipment. So, exercise your muscles of authority and see victory and miracles come to pass.

Have a
JESUS
Filled Day

A DAY
FILLED WITH
VICTORY

DAILY CONFESSION

Thank You, Lord, that I live all of my days filled with victory. Thank You that I am able to overcome every storm that comes my way, as I trust in You. I am so glad that You, oh God, are bigger than any problem that I will ever face. Thank You that I don't have to deal with my struggles on my own. I place them in Your hands, giving You permission to handle every situation. Thank You Lord, that as I keep pressing forward in the midst of every trial, that I speak Your Word and see victory in every area of my life.

Today, *I have A Day Filled with Victory!*

A DAY
FILLED WITH
MIRACLES

"Jesus said unto him, 'Rise, take up your bed and walk.'" —JOHN 5:8

The Bible tells us of many miracles Jesus performed. We are so glad there is no limit to the miracles Jesus wants to perform for all of us. The greatest miracle is salvation. *When you ask Jesus into your heart as your Lord and Savior, it is the greatest miracle in your life.* If you do not know Jesus as your Savior, we pray you will ask Him into your heart today and let Him fill you with the miracle of salvation.

FAMILY MIRACLES

After Ann and I rededicated our lives to Jesus, we had many days filled with miracles. Our youngest daughter was born with a defect in her hips and legs. She was unable to walk straight and unable run. She had to wear braces and the doctors said she would not be able to participate in any sports. However, the Lord miraculously healed her. She later became a cheerleader and has continually participated in many different sports.

When I had a heart attack, the doctors said I had damage to the back of my heart. With my wife, family, and others praying for a miracle, the Lord healed and repaired my heart.

> ". . . by His wounds you have been healed."
> —1 PETER 2:24 (NIV)

After my mother-in-law died of breast cancer in 1972, Ann began to have mammograms every year and her reports were always good. However, in November of 1989 her report was different.

The doctor called her immediately to have a biopsy because he was concerned. Then that report came, we were no longer destroyed from a lack of knowledge (Hosea 4:6). We recommitted our lives to the Lord Jesus. We learned it was God's will to heal and we had already seen many miracles in our family, including my recovery from a heart attack, miracles in our children's lives, answers to prayers in business, and miracles in many other areas.

We began to pray before we went to the hospital for the biopsy. We both had peace because we knew God had already paid the price for her healing. When the biopsy was done, they discovered there were two types of cancer in her breast. One of them was a very fast growing type, and the doctor recommended surgery right away. Ann had peace about the surgery because she already knew the Lord Jesus would go through it with her and she would have a quick recovery. After surgery, the doctor suggested that she see an oncologist to have radiation, chemotherapy, or both. However, she did not see an oncologist, nor did she take radiation or chemotherapy, and she has been cancer free for over sixteen years.

One month and one day after Ann's surgery, one of our sons was accidentally shot in a hunting accident by his best friend. The doctors did not expect him to live because of the severity of the gunshot wound to the chest and the loss of so much blood before he arrived at the hospital. However, Ann and I, our son's wife, and all of our families came together with prayer and faith believing for his healing. We were strong in our faith in God and His promises. We knew our son would not die but live to declare the works of God. Jesus Christ miraculously healed him. After two weeks, he walked out of the hospital without surgery.

In 1990, three months after the events surrounding our son, one of my uncles was shot by a young man on drugs who was attempting to rob him while he was at a stop sign. He was in intensive care for thirty-two days, and the doctor had to use shock treatments on his heart several times. They said there was no way he would live because of the unusually high doses of the antibiotics used, to eliminate the infection, would likely kill him.

We had seen Jesus move in our family already, and we knew the promises of God.

That uncle was more than just an uncle to me. When my mother died at an early age in my life, he helped to raise me. It was important for me to believe the report of the Lord and not the report of the doctors. As family and friends continued to believe and pray for him, all the doctors and nurses were shocked when God miraculously healed him.

Several years later, my wife and I had a head on collision with a truck, and our car was totaled. I was pinned in the car and had to be cut out of the wreckage. When the paramedics diagnosed my physical condition, they discovered that I had a broken arm. Ann experienced some bruising on her chest from the seatbelt, but the paramedics seemed to be focused on my injuries. While we were being rushed to the hospital, Ann began to pray that the Lord would miraculously heal my broken bones and cause them to come into proper alignment. By the time we arrived at the hospital, I sensed that I had received a miraculous touch of the Lord throughout my body. After being examined at the hospital, it was concluded that I did not have one broken bone in my body. What *A Day Filled with Miracles* that was!

Throughout the years, each of our five children have experienced major automobile accidents without serious injury. We thank the Lord Jesus Christ for every single miracle. The miracles in our lives have encouraged family members and friends to remember, "'. . . for with God all things are possible,'" (Mark 10:27). Our God is no different today than He has ever been. The same God that parted the Red Sea so that His people could walk across on dry ground (Exodus 14) is the

> ". . . with God all things are possible." —MATTHEW 19: 26 (NIV)

same God that can make a way where there seems to be no way for you today. The same God that was with the three Hebrew young men when they were thrown into a fiery furnace (Daniel 3) is the same God that can miraculously bring you through any fiery trial you are thrown into.

The same God that healed "all those who were afflicted," (Matthew 4:24 HCSB) is the same God that can heal your body today. The same God that turned five loaves and two fish into a meal for 5,000 (Matthew 14) is the same God that can provide for your every need today. A Jesus Filled Day is always *A Day Filled with Miracles,* whether large or small. Believe Him today for whatever miracle you need. Know that God's grace includes the very miracle you need at this moment. Don't miss out on the divine favor you desire!

A DAY
FILLED WITH
MIRACLES

DAILY CONFESSION

Thank You, Lord, for being the same yesterday, today, and forever. The same miracles that You displayed 2,000 years ago are the same miracles that You want to display in my life today. No matter what the circumstance in my life demands, You are a miracle-working Savior. With You, all things are possible.

Today, *I have A Day Filled with Miracles!*

A DAY
FILLED WITH
FAVOR

"... living the good life which He prearranged
and made ready for us to live."
—EPHESIANS 2:10 (AMP)

Do you know that God knew you before you
were born? He knew you before your parents knew
each other. He has a unique plan and purpose for
your life. The God that we serve is a great God.
Ephesians 3:20 says that He is able to do in, and
through you, something greater than anything you
could imagine or think. What a God!

FAVOR BRINGS THE PLANS OF GOD

"And so find favor and high esteem in the sight
of God and man. Trust in the Lord with all your
heart, and lean not on your own understanding;

> "For He chose us in Him before the creation of the world to be holy and blameless in His sight."
> —EPHESIANS 1:4 (NIV)

in all your ways acknowledge Him, and He shall direct your paths," (Proverbs 3:4-6 NKJV). That Scripture does not say a little of your heart, nor does it say most of your heart. You have to trust Him with all of your heart. If you want God's favor in your life, be open to His plan.

Many times your natural reaction is to trust God, but only to a certain extent. People feel that if they can just maintain a little bit of control in their life, then they can help God. Unfortunately, that lack of trust brings you into difficult situations where you are not able to operate with the favor of God.

> "And the angel came in unto her, and said, Hail, thou that art highly favoured, the Lord is with thee: blessed art thou among women."
> —LUKE 1:28

In Luke 1:26-38, God sent the angel, Gabriel, to deliver a message to a young girl named Mary. Gabriel told her that she was highly favored and the Lord was with her to complete His plan. She questioned the angel by asking him how what he said could come to pass since she was a virgin. The angel told Mary that the Holy Spirit would come upon her and she would be with child. "Then Mary said, 'Behold the maidservant of the Lord! Let it be to me according to your word.' And the angel departed from her," (v. 38).

Mary was open to the plan of God. She submitted completely to God's will. She trusted Him to bring the impossible to pass, knowing that nothing was impossi-

> "For nothing is impossible with God."
> —LUKE 1:37 (NLT)

ble with God. After one divine encounter with the Holy Spirit, Mary stepped into her purpose that was ordained for her before the foundation of the world.

She was favored over all women to carry and give birth to the Messiah, the Son of God. She accepted the favor of God on her life above everything else. God's will for her life was more important than her reputation, her plans, the shame of being an unwed mother, or the risk of being stoned to death. What are you willing to give up in order to have a day filled with God's favor? Mary was willing to give up an ordinary day for an extraordinary day. From a certain perspective, that was the first time an individual truly experienced a Jesus Filled Day. Mary accepted the favor of the Lord on her life and the result was the implanting of a baby in her womb who would be named *Jesus*.

You need to respond and believe in that same manner concerning the calling on your life. By declaring, "So be it unto me," you receive God's plan and favor for your life. When you accept that Word and act upon it, you will see the favor of God bless your life. In the Bible, you find the word "favor" very closely related to the word "grace." In fact, the word grace literally means *the unmerited divine favor and gift of God.* That knowledge helps people understand that they can never buy, or earn, God's gift of favor. Favor is a gift that God gives to everyone who comes into a saving knowledge of Jesus Christ.

Each morning as you awake, declare, *"God, let Your Word come to pass in my life today. Let me know Your grace (favor and blessing) on my life so that I may be able to do Your will."* While some individuals may wake up today with a negative or grumpy attitude, you need to have confidence that God's Word promises to give you favor today. Choosing to be positive, instead of negative, is an expression of faith in God to give you what you need when you need it. There are no delays with God. We have heard it said that God is never too early, never too late, and He is always on time.

DELAYS

In our church, we have a young man who came to the United States from Africa. However, he came to America with his fiancée still overseas. A short while after living in America, he went back to Africa to marry his fiancée and bring her back with him to America. Because of family traditions, there were many delays before the marriage could take place. Finally, they were able to wed, but the delays in time meant that he had to return to America shortly after their wedding, a few days before his visa would expire. With her paperwork in order, he fully expected his wife to receive her visa and join him in America quickly. Shortly after the young man arrived in the United States, he learned that his wife had become pregnant before he left Africa. Their baby was born nine months later, but her visa had still not been granted.

Continually, the immigration officer refused to grant her a visa. Each time she applied meant more money and more time to wait on the results. Days turned into months and months turned into a year. During that time, we stood in agreement with him that no matter what it looked like, God had heard our petitions and would grant our request.

Finally, after a year had passed, his faith was beginning to waiver. He was so discouraged in his spirit that he was willing to adopt the ways of other Africans who were in a similar position.

"Again I say to you, if two of you agree on earth about anything they ask, it will be done for them by my Father in heaven."
—MATTHEW 18:19 (ESV)

Initially, he would be willing to leave the baby in Africa, being content to only have his wife in America, and hoping to send for his newborn son some time in the future. Ann and I immediately corrected his thinking and instructed him to change his words. We encouraged him and prayed with him. We agreed to believe that his son would be able to come at the same time as his wife. We encouraged him to believe that it was God's plan for his entire family to be in America. The favor of God would be manifested even if God had to provide a different officer at the Embassy who would give his wife and son favor, granting both visas.

Not long after we prayed, a new immigration officer took the place of the first individual. The new officer was baffled as to why a normally speedy process took over a year. That officer immediately granted the young man's wife and son their visas, and they were able to join him in America. That was *A Day Filled with Favor!* One touch of God's favor can turn everything around so quickly.

Have a
JESUS
Filled Day

A DAY
FILLED WITH
FAVOR

DAILY CONFESSION

Thank You, Lord, that I walk in Your favor. You are a great God and have wonderful plans for my life. I trust You with all of my heart and do not lean on my own understanding. I know You have my best interest in Your heart. I expect doors to open and people to work on my behalf, according to the plans You have for my life. Everything works for the good in my life because I love You and am called according to Your purpose.

Today, I have *A Day Filled with Favor!*

CHAPTER SEVEN

A DAY
FILLED WITH
SATISFACTION

". . . And My people shall be satisfied with
My goodness, saith the Lord."
—JEREMIAH 31:14

God desires to satisfy all needs which will
empower believers to live and serve the Lord.
He wants to satisfy every part of you: spirit,
soul, and body. God
knows that the body
wants to be satis-
fied with things that
please the body;
such as food, cloth-
ing, and shelter. He

"Who satisfies your de-
sires with good things . . ."
—PSALM 103:5 (NIV)

knows that the soul wants to be satisfied with
knowledge, wisdom, and understanding. He
even knows that our spirit wants be satisfied

with spiritual things, such as the Word of God and prayer. He knows because He is the source of life, the Creator.

INSTANT GRATIFICATION PROVIDES TEMPORARY SATISFACTION

There are numerous examples in the Bible that show us how instant gratification will only provide temporary satisfaction. David's desire for Bathsheba provided him with temporary satisfaction, but later led to murder (2 Samuel 11).

Esau was tricked out of his birthright by Jacob because he desired to be satisfied with food (Genesis 27). Lot's wife still desired to receive instant gratification from the world, but when she looked back, it destroyed her (Genesis 19). A hasty decision to fill a temporary satisfaction can lead to the destruction of lives and family relationships.

> "You open Your hand and satisfy the desire of every living thing."
> —PSALM 145:16 (NIV)

Earthly things are temporary, but eternity is forever. Obtaining things on earth is only for a season, but losing your soul is forever. Earthly satisfaction is just for a moment. The Bible says in Matthew 16:26 (NKJV), "For what profit is it to a man if he gains the whole world, and loses his own soul? Or what will a man give in exchange for his soul?" The word "want" is defined as "to desire greatly or to request the presence of." Our spirit desires greatly, or requests the presence of, the things that please or satisfy God; people saved and lives transformed into His image.

Have you come to a place where you desire to be satisfied with the things of God? Do you desire, above everything else, for Jesus to satisfy every area of your life? If you do, you must be willing to seek Jesus with all of your heart. Look at this simple, yet powerful statement Jesus made in Matthew 6:31-33 (KJV), "Therefore take no thought, saying, What shall we eat? or, What shall we drink? or, Wherewithal shall we be clothed? (For after all these things do the Gentiles seek:) for your heavenly Father knoweth that ye have need of all these things. But seek ye first the kingdom of God, and his righteousness; and all these things shall be added unto you."

> "Blessed are you who hunger now, for you will be satisfied." —LUKE 6:21 (NIV)

THROUGHOUT YOUR LIFE, WHAT SATISFIES YOU CHANGES

During the course of your life, the things that satisfy you change. You arc going to want something more or something different than you already have. At one season in your life you might have wanted a two bedroom house, but now you want a four bedroom house. Once you wanted a four door, green Honda. Now, you want a two door, red Corvette. You might have desired a job that paid twenty thousand dollars per year. Now you desire a job that pays sixty thousand dollars per year. Whatever material and worldly things you obtain will only satisfy you for a short period of time.

God knows that material things can only provide temporary satisfaction. Without Him, things of the world will not satisfy you. But in a relationship with Him, you are truly satisfied as you seek the kingdom of God, which includes spending time in His presence and fulfilling His will for your life. To have *A Day Filled with Satisfaction*, you must allow your life to be completely open to everything that Jesus has to offer to you. So many people do not want to accept Christ in His fullness. They only want to accept a portion of Jesus. However, Jesus does not just want to fill up a room, but the whole house of your life. It is easy to compartmentalize your relationship with God.

You will let Him have lordship over Sundays but not your weekdays. You will let Him govern your prayer time but not what entertainment you choose to view. You will let Him lead your time in Bible Study, but you won't let Him be the leader of your home and your marriage. Jesus wants to be a part of everything in your life; the big things and the small things.

If you really desire something, you will go to great extremes to get it. You will do things that you normally would not do. You will change, move, put aside, or cast away anything that will stop or hinder you. For example, if a man desires a relationship with a certain woman, he will dress different, talk different, and even change his hairstyle if it means he can have her in his life. The same is true about a woman. If you sincerely want a relationship, then you will go after it.

Do you remember how determined you were to have that new car, new home, new job, or buy that new computer? You knew it was possible, so you went after it. It was worth the price to you. You began to meditate on having it, you believed that it was yours, you spoke about it, and then you went after it. After you got it, you felt satisfied.

If you are going to have a Jesus Filled Day, you have to be very determined. Start seeing it, meditating about it, and believing it. Then, speak it, expect it, and go after it! Go in the power of the Holy Spirit because it will never be by your efforts alone.

WHAT TYPE OF RELATIONSHIP
DO YOU SEEK?

If you live with a person but never spend time with them, you will never truly know them. I have seen married couples live together for twenty years or more and still not know each other. Why do you think they end up in divorce? They do not spend time together. They do not communicate with each other.

In the Word of God, there are examples of individuals who knew God well because they spent time with Him. There are also other examples of individuals who didn't know God because they didn't spend time with Him. The book of Genesis tells about a man named Lot, the nephew of Abraham. Lot was familiar with Jehovah God because Abraham had a great level of communication with God. However, there is nowhere in Scripture that gives any indication that Lot had communication with God on his own. Eventually, the time came for Lot and Abraham to part ways. Abraham followed the plan of God while Lot followed his own desires for personal satisfaction. As time went by, Abraham received complete satisfaction from God Almighty, while Lot lived among perversion and sin. Ultimately, Lot had to abandon his home, lost his wife, and his daughters ended up committing incestuous acts with him.

> "And the Lord spake unto Moses face to face, as a man speaketh to his friend . . ."
> —EXODUS 33:11

Moses was a man who experienced the miracles that God performed to bring satisfaction to His people. He witnessed God satisfy the body by supernaturally providing bread, water, and shelter (Exodus 13-16). Most of all, he supernaturally experienced God's presence, face to face (Exodus 33).

God is no respecter of persons. Like Moses, you can also have an intimate relationship with God. He does not just want to live in you. He wants you to talk to Him and to have a relationship with Him. He desires for you to draw close to Him so that you can be satisfied with His goodness and peace.

A DAY
FILLED WITH
SATISFACTION

DAILY CONFESSION

Thank You, Lord, that Your desire is to satisfy me. I do not seek instant gratification but allow You to satisfy every need that I have. I do not push You out of any area of my life. Instead, I seek to have an intimate friendship and relationship with You, allowing me to be satisfied with Your goodness.

Today, I have *A Day Filled with Satisfaction!*

CHAPTER EIGHT

A DAY
FILLED WITH
PEACE

"Thou wilt keep him in perfect peace, whose mind is stayed on thee: because he trusteth in thee." —ISAIAH 26:3

If you seek Jesus, the Prince of Peace, He will fill your day with His peace. John 14:27 (ESV) says, "Peace I leave with you, My peace I give to you; not as the world gives, do I give to you. Let not your heart be troubled, neither let it be afraid."

YOU CAN CAST YOUR BURDENS ON JESUS

God knows the root of your problems, and He knows how to solve every one of them. On your own, you cannot handle them with a great deal of success. He wants to handle them for you because He never intended for you to carry a heavy load. First Peter 5:7 (NIV), affirms you to, "Cast all your anxiety on Him because He cares for you." Jesus desires to be your burden bearer. Jesus, Himself, said these words in Matthew 11:29-30, "Take My yoke upon you and learn from Me, for I am gentle and humble in heart, and you will find rest for your souls. For My yoke is easy and My burden is light."

Learning to fill our days with peace has enabled us to remain steadfast, even in the midst of difficult circumstances. For example, some time ago one of our adult sons was attacked by a longhorned cow. Goring and throwing him with its horns, the cow caused significant physical damage. The surgeon repaired our son's torn body, but he warned us that lifelong complications could occur, such as the inability to produce more children.

> "Casting all your care upon him; for he careth for you."
> —1 PETER 5:7

However, Jesus performed a miracle and later our son had another child. Throughout that ordeal, we focused on the Word of God and He gave us perfect peace. He made all of us; therefore, He knows we cannot carry heavy burdens. We need to cast all the cares of yesterday, today, and tomorrow on the Lord. He will give us perfect peace when our minds are focused on Him, not on our problems. We need to lay our burdens at the nail pierced feet of Jesus and leave them there.

Yes, the wind of life may blow and your boat may be tossed in the sea, but you can be anchored in Him. An *anchor* is a large piece of metal tied to a ship or boat to keep it stationary in the water. If you let Jesus be the anchor of your life, the worldly things around you will only have limited influence. As the waves roll by, you might bounce around in the water, bobbing up and down. However, you will stand firm amidst everything going on around you when Jesus is your anchor. That is the peace available to you when you trust Him in all you do. An example can be found in Hebrews 6:19, where Paul uses an anchor to indicate the stability of God's promise of salvation to those who believe in Him. Regardless of what is going on around you, God will provide comfort.

KEEP YOURSELF CHARGED UP

When a car is not started on a regular basis, the battery will lose its charge. Eventually, the battery will die, not being able to hold any charge what-

> "We have this hope as an anchor for the soul, firm and secure . . ."
> —HEBREWS 6:19 (NIV)

soever. Although a car can go several days without being started, it is always better to start it often to keep the battery charged.

In Exodus 16 of the Old Testament, after Moses led God's people out of Egypt, God began to feed them with a food called "manna." The people of

God were instructed to get fresh manna every day. It came to them every morning except the Sabbath, appearing on the ground. A double amount could be gathered to last through the Sabbath.

Some of the people ignored God's instruction to go out every morning to receive the new food and, instead, tried to take more than a day's worth of manna. The manna they took became rotten and filled with worms. God's words were very clear. The people needed to obtain their food every single day. In the same way, your spirit was meant to be charged every day.

> "However, when He, the Spirit of truth, has come, He will guide you into all truth ..." —JOHN 16:13 (WEB)

What you received yesterday isn't enough for today. You must charge your spirit every day by giving God praise and thanksgiving, spending time in prayer, and reading the Bible.

Some people enjoy a cup of coffee in the morning while others might prefer a walk. I choose to start my day by renewing my mind in the Spirit and entering into the presence of the Lord, asking Him to direct my path. Each morning, when I get out of bed, I get up excited about God. I'm excited that God wants to do something good for me that day. He is just waiting for me to wake up so that He can bless me. He wants to bless me with

His presence, His love, and His wonderful peace. He wants to do the same for you. He wants to fill your day with His peace, and He wants to give you guidance.

A DAY
FILLED WITH
PEACE

DAILY CONFESSION

Thank You, Lord, that I have the ability to cast every burden, every concern, every worry, and every fear on Your shoulders. In return, You give me peace that passes my understanding. Trials and tests may come, but I choose to remain anchored in You, oh Lord. You hold me secure as I find my peace in You.

Today, *I have A Day Filled with Peace!*

A DAY
FILLED WITH
GUIDANCE

"The Lord will guide you continually,
And satisfy your soul in drought, And strengthen
your bones; you shall be like a watered garden,
And like a spring of water, whose waters do not
fail." —ISAIAH 58:11 (NKJV)

It is so important to walk with God daily. We
know that Enoch walked with God (Genesis 5:22-
24), and Noah walked with God (Genesis 6:9).
Both men lived a righteous life before God. They
had a relationship with God. Their life and conversation pleased Him.

If you walk with Jesus daily, He will guide your
footsteps and keep you from falling. He will never
lead you down the wrong path. Psalm 37:23 says,
"The steps of a good man are ordered by the Lord,
and He delights in his way." Every single person

that ever lives on this earth has a purpose. You must keep your purpose in mind when you are walking with God, never giving up, no matter what the situation.

Walking in the will of the Father does not mean you will not have any difficulties. However, no matter the difficulties you encounter, He will see you through them all. In John 16:33, Jesus said, ". . . In the world you will have tribulation; but be of good cheer, I have overcome the world." That truth is something to be excited about. There is another promise given to us that we see in Psalm 84:11, where it says that there will be no good thing that He will withhold from them whose walk is blameless. Regardless if it is your natural walk or your spiritual walk, God will fill your life with guidance.

Your trust must be in the Lord, not in a lawyer, a doctor, a job, or even your bank account. First Timothy 6:17 says that God has given us all things to enjoy. A lawyer can be a blessing. A doctor can be of great help. A job can be a source of comfort and security. Thank God that you have them available to you if you need them. Yet still, your trust needs to be in the Lord.

A JESUS FILLED DAY IS A DAY FULL OF TRUST

Do you realize how important it is that you trust God? If you really trust Him, you will act according to the truth He has revealed to you. When you trust in the Lord Jesus, He will never lead you down the wrong path. You cannot have a Jesus Filled Day if you do not trust Him for direction to provide whatever you need.

If you cannot trust someone, you cannot believe what he or she says. You cannot depend on their words because they have proven that their words are not trustworthy. They might have lied to you or someone you know. They might have gone back on what they said.

God has never lied. In fact, the Bible tells us that God *cannot* lie (Titus 1:2, Hebrews 6:18). God will never go back on His Word. Every word that God has spoken has come to pass. You have every reason to trust and have faith in God.

The Bible says, ". . . if you have faith and do not doubt . . . " (Matthew 21:21 NIV). In other words, you must cast all of your cares upon Jesus because He cares for you. You have to trust Him and believe by faith. When you connect trust and faith together, He will guide you in the way you should go. You will see the things of the Lord manifest in your heart and in your life. When things do not look right, when things do not sound right, when things do not even feel right, just trust in Him.

Have you noticed how children trust people? Their trust is instinctive, but can easily be broken by someone who does not follow through with their word. For example, if you tell a child to jump off the bed and you fail to catch them, their trust in you will decrease. If they end up injured, be

> "So Jesus answered and said unto them, 'Verily, I say unto you, if you have faith, and not doubt..."
>
> —MATTHEW 21:21

assured, they will not jump if you ask them again. Why? Fear will come to their mind. They do not have confidence in what you say. They will not follow your directions with trust.

When you trust in the Word of the Lord Jesus Christ, it is a foundation not built by human hands. *It is a solid foundation.* Matthew 7:24 says, "Therefore whoever hears these sayings of Mine, and does them, I will liken him to a wise man who built his house on the rock." The Word of the Lord is eternal. It is sure. When He speaks, it is so.

You might say, "I could enjoy this day if I did not have to go to work. I could enjoy this day if I had more money. I could enjoy this day if I did not have sickness in my body." Do not let the things of this world run down your spiritual battery. Unfortunately, we all face difficulties and challenges in our lives. No matter how hopeless your situation may be right now, you can still have a Jesus Filled Day because it is a choice.

Everyday you make choices that determine the direction of your day. Everyday you determine the road in life you will travel. Sometimes your choices lead to a road that is smooth, while other times your choices lead to a road that is bumpy. But

Have a
JESUS
Filled Day

your choices will lead to whatever destination you choose. Choose to have a Jesus Filled Day. You may have to make a decision about your life and it may not please those around you. You have to make a choice everyday not to let anything frustrate, discourage, or cause you to lose your joy.

Certainly, you will encounter opportunities to become frustrated, angry, or upset. However, you have the ability to choose how you respond to those situations; you can choose not to respond in a negative fashion. You can choose to respond with a positive confession that states, by faith, you are having a good day, despite your circumstances.

I challenge you to make a decision to fill up each day with Christ, and let Him guide you in every area. Each day you should confess, "Lord you are my strength, my refuge, my strong tower, my peace, my healer, my guide, and my fortress." Statements like that should fill your day; words that bless Jesus, words that praise Him, and words that let Him guide your footsteps.

> "The steps of a good man are ordered by the LORD: and he delighteth in his way. Though he fall, he shall not be utterly cast down: for the LORD upholdeth him with his hand."
> —PSALM 37:23-24 (NIV)

If you put God first, He will orchestrate your day so that you will be successful in everything you do. He knows everything that will happen each day, whether good or bad. If you spend time with Him, He will prepare you for each day. Read His Word, pray, and worship Him. Why? So you can enjoy His presence, and expect to enjoy your day.

Think of Mary and Joseph in the New Testament. More than likely, they had plans for the direction of their lives. Their plans had to change when the Holy Spirit came upon Mary and she conceived Jesus. They had to change their direction in order to fulfill the plan of God for their lives.

A PERSONAL GUIDE

Years ago, when my family and I had the opportunity to visit Israel, we toured with a guide. He was there every morning waiting for us to get on the bus. We could ask him any question pertaining to the tour and he would answer us, explaining all the different aspects of the tour's historical locations. How wonderful it was to be and walk, where Jesus walked.

Without a guide, we would not have gone to Israel. We would not have been able to find our way around that area of land without him. We could have purchased a map, but it would have done little to provide the direction for us that a personal guide was able to offer. In your spiritual life, you have a personal guide. That's what the Holy Spirit wants to be to you. He wants to be your individual guide. He wants to guide you personally. He wants to take you from where you are to where you are supposed to be. So many people won't listen to a guide because they think they know the best direction for their life. The Lord wants to guide and direct you in every aspect of your life, each and every day.

The Bible talks about the blind leading the blind (Matthew 15:14). I have a full understanding of leading the natural blind. When I was a young boy, there was a blind man called "Blind Bill" in our church. I was his guide at the church. He would place his hand on my shoulder and when we came to a step, he could feel me go up the step and he would follow me, never missing a step. Why? Because he was touching me. He was in tune and in touch with what was going on with his guide. "Blind Bill" knew he couldn't see. He knew if he let go of me he would be lost in darkness.

When you let go of the Holy Spirit, you are in darkness. Many times people come to the place where they think they can do whatever they want to do. They don't think they need Jesus. They don't think they need to be led by the Holy Spirit. They don't think they need to depend on the Father. In reality, quite the opposite situation is vital for their lives. They need guidance from Jesus today more than ever. They need the Spirit of God like never before. They need the understanding of His presence and His glory like never before. You are going to have to start from where you are right now and depend upon His guidance.

Depend upon Him. *Guidance* is an act or instance of guiding. A *guide* is one who leads the way, directs, or advises. Spiritual guidance is about purpose and destiny. It is about His presence and His glory. In Luke 4:1-13, the devil wanted to stop Jesus. He wanted to stop His destiny and His purpose.

What did Jesus say to respond to the temptation of Satan? ". . . 'Get behind Me, Satan!' . . ." (v. 8). If the devil could have stopped Jesus, he could have stopped the purpose and the destiny, the presence and the glory of Almighty God from manifesting in your life. The devil wants to stop the purpose in your life. Therefore, say "No" to the devil and say "Yes" to God, especially when you are seeking guidance.

> "Whenever he brings out his own sheep, he goes before them, and the sheep follow him, for they know his voice."
> —JOHN 10:4 (WEB)

Receiving proper guidance and direction are key ingredients to help you receive what is rightfully and justly yours. It is very important that you do not let anything stop you. Jesus did not let anything stop Him. When God speaks to you, He does so from where you are now, by providing guidance about where you are headed.

The Lord speaks about the direction for you to travel, where you are supposed to go, and what you are supposed to do. Your past is not involved. Sometimes, on the road of your life, the past can act like a stop sign. When you stop, there is a chance for you to become confused and go the wrong direction. The stop sign was not put there by God. It was put there by the devil.

However, there are stop signs that the Lord puts in your path. That is why you have to be in tune with Him. The Bible says His sheep know His voice (John 10:3-5). The devil is always bringing up your past so that you will be distracted from God's plan for your life. Don't let your past get in the way of the future that the Lord wants to guide you toward. What you did in the past is already over.

In order to move ahead in the things of God by His guidance, take your past and let it be an encouragement to you, regardless if your past is good or bad. We all must realize how dependent we should be on the Lord for guidance. Life is like a vapor; here today, gone tomorrow. Therefore, it is very urgent that you receive guidance from Him in every part of your life so you do not stumble or fall.

People need a road map for guidance. What is the road map for living a life knowing that you are being guided by God? Guidance for the believer is found in the Word of God. Some people try to go through life without ever reading the Bible. The Word of God will guide you because it has the answer for every situation in your life. The Bible says, he will guide you into all truth... - John 16:13 (WEB) Therefore, He is guiding you to where you need to be at the time you need to be there. People need to speak the promises of God's Word, confessing, "I'm under the Word of God. He is my Director, my Father is my Guide."

Let Him fill every day of your life with His *guidance*! The secret to guidance is your relationship to the *Guide*, the Lord Jesus. He will give you purpose and vision for life.

A DAY
FILLED WITH
GUIDANCE

DAILY CONFESSION

Thank You, Lord, that my steps are ordered by You. I don't place my trust in money, a man, or any other type of security. I rely completely on You. You are trustworthy, and I have faith in You and Your Word. Lord, You are my strength, my refuge, my strong tower, my peace, my healer, and my fortress. Thank You, Lord, that You are my guide. You lead, guide, and direct every step I take.

Today, *I have A Day Filled with Guidance!*

A DAY

FILLED WITH

VISION

"While we look not at the things which are seen,
but at the things which are not seen;
for the things which are seen are temporal,
but the things which are not seen are eternal."
—2 CORINTHIANS 4:18

Vision is being able to see. If you are going to have a Jesus Filled Day you have to see through the "eyes of faith" – seeing the impossible as possible. The Biblical definition of faith is "Now faith is the substance of things hoped for, the evidence of things not seen," (Hebrews 11:1). Even though you do not see what you desire with your natural eyes, your spiritual vision and revelation believes that what you desire will come to pass as His Word promises. Keep your focus and sense of purpose as you walk with God. Without a sense of purpose, a vision or goal set before you, you will end up defeated on the road of life. Without vision, you will end up quitting during hard times. Do not focus on your circumstances. Instead, focus on Jesus.

VISION KEEPS US FOCUSED

"Where there is no vision [no revelation of God and His word], the people are unrestrained . . ."
—PROVERBS 29:18 (AMP)

"Where there is no vision, the people perish . . ." (Proverbs 29:18 KJV). Another way of understanding that verse is that if there is no vision, people will lose hope. Have you lost hope, or are you ready to give up? Do you feel that what you have been waiting for will never come to pass, or that you will never possess the promise?

We would like to remind you of Abram. His story can be found in the book of Genesis in the Old Testament. Just when Abram was about to lose hope of ever having a son, God appeared to him in a vision promising that his descendants would be too numerous to imagine (Genesis 15:4-5, 22:17). God promised that his descendants would be like the stars in the sky or the grains of sand on the seashore, too many to count. At the age of ninety-nine God changed his name to Abraham, meaning father of many nations. Abraham had many opportunities to give up. When he was seventy-five, eighty-five, and even ninety years old, he still did not have a son with Sarah. People may have whispered behind his back that he and Sarah were too old to have a child.

Most likely their bodies showed physical signs of their age, but Abraham and Sarah chose to believe God's vision for their lives. In a similar fashion, your family may tell you that God's promises to you will never happen. Your friends may tell you to throw in the towel. People tend to have all sorts of reasons why they believe you will never receive the promises. They base their judgments on your age, height, weight, race, gender, or some other physical feature.

At the age of one hundred years old, Abraham had a son. Wow! God's blessings are well beyond our imaginations. If you believe, confess, and stay focused on the vision, you will flourish. In other words, you will prosper. You will see and receive things that others do not.

THINGS ARE NOT ALWAYS THE WAY THEY LOOK

Many years ago, Ann and I were in Orlando, Florida. While we were there, Ann wanted to do some shopping. That particular time, I decided to wait for her in the car. While she was in the store, a couple came out of the store and got into a car. Suddenly, they got out of that car and speedily made their way to another car identical to the one they had just left. Apparently, the first car looked like their car and may have even felt like their car but when they tried to start it, it would not start. Someone had left the vehicle unlocked, and when they got in it, they thought it was their car. I was reminded that things are not always the way they appear.

Many people are getting into the wrong vehicle in life. The wrong vehicle to you might be believing the words of the devil. Do you know that the devil is a liar? Do you realize that if he is talking, he is lying? God called him the father of all lies (John 8:44). So, whose vision are you going to believe for your life? You can either believe God and His Word, or the devil and his lies.

> ". . . for there is no truth in him. When he lies, he speaks his native language, for he is a liar and the father of lies."
> —JOHN 8:44 (NIV)

We encourage you to look at the Word of God and what His vision is for your situation. Say what the Word says: ". . . And by His stripes we are healed," (Isaiah 53:5 NIV). You're not going to try to receive your healing. You are *already* healed. You are blessed coming and going, and everything you put your hand to is blessed.

You may not feel it. You may not look like it. But believe what the Word of God says about you. Do not be moved by what you see. Do not be moved by what you hear. Only be moved by what you believe as the Holy Spirit teaches, reveals, and leads you. You must look through eyes of faith and start seeing the vision of the real you: happy, healthy, and whole. That means that even when your situation looks hopeless, put faith to work and see the results. When you face crises in your life, hold onto your faith in Jesus and keep your vision fixed on the promises of God's Word.

A DAY
FILLED WITH
VISION

DAILY CONFESSION

Today, Lord, I see through the eyes of faith. I believe the impossible is possible through You. No matter what the signs around are telling me, I hold to the promises of Your Word. I believe Your Word is truth that is above the opinions of man and the circumstances I observe. I choose to have vision. I choose to see myself and the condition of my life the way that You reveal it to me.

Today, *I have A Day Filled with Vision!*

A DAY

FILLED WITH

ABUNDANCE

"... I have come that they may have life,
and that they might have life, and that
they might have it more abundantly."

—JOHN 10:10

If you could change your life so it would be
filled with joy and peace in every area, would you
change it? So many people are unhappy with their
lives. Far too often, the cares of life have robbed
them of joy, peace, wealth, and even their health.

Some people become consumed with the cares
of this life; what they are going to eat, what they
are going to wear, how they are going to pay their
bills, or where they are going to work. Other people
are consumed with commitments, business meet-
ings, doctor's appointments, their children's activi-

ties, and taking care of the family. The pressures can seem overwhelming.

> "The thief comes only to steal and kill and destroy; I have come that they may have life, and have it to the full."
>
> —JOHN 10:10 (NIV)

One of the reasons that Jesus came was to relieve the pressure. John 10:10 says, "The thief does not come except to steal, and to kill, and to destroy. I have come that they may have life, and that they may have it more abundantly." He came that you would have an abundant life.

Abundant means having something in plentiful supply: full, ample, more than enough, surplus, or overflowing. His promise is that you enjoy life everyday and live life in abundance. In other words, you can have a day filled with His abundance. That begins with spiritual blessings, but includes more. The very nature of God is that you have goodness in so much abundance that it overflows into every part of your life. Despite being unworthy of His grace, you should ask Him to bless you abundantly. It is God's nature to bless His people. What is a day filled with God's abundance? It is a day you live life to its fullest. It is a day filled with the presence of Jesus. When Jesus fills your day, there is no room for anything else; no room for doubt, fear, defeat, envy, strife, unforgiveness, jealousy, lack, or loneliness. Those negative elements of life are the exact opposite of the promises of a life that is filled with Jesus. Romans 14:17 tells us, "for the kingdom of God is . . . righteousness and peace and joy in the Holy Spirit." Having those attributes operating in your life allows you to experience the kind of day God wants for you!

Answer this question: Why not you? Stop and think about it. It is possible for every person to have a Jesus Filled Day.

> "For with God nothing shall be impossible."
> —LUKE 1:37

That type of life is not reserved for those who have nothing to do and no cares in this world. A Day Filled with Abundance is available to every believer. Remember, with God nothing is impossible (Luke 1:37). It might take a little more time to achieve, but it will be worth it. God wants an abundant life for you. As mentioned earlier, abundance means full or more than enough. When you are full of Christ Jesus, you will speak of the things of God. You will speak the promises that God has given you.

WHEN THE WORD IS ABIDING IN YOU

Believe in your heart that those promises belong to you. You cannot just speak the Word and expect it to come to pass. The Bible says: " . . . For out of the abundance of the heart the mouth speaks," (Matthew 12:34). Your words have power when you believe the Word of God with all of your heart. The Scriptures declare: "If ye abide in me, and my words abide in you, ye shall ask what ye will, and it shall be done unto you," (John 15:7). The key words in that verse come at the beginning where Jesus declares the importance of a relationship with Him and a relationship with His Word. When the Word of God is deeply rooted inside of you, you are at a place where you have the attention of the Lord Jesus. He knows everything you need. He says that He will supply your every need and give you the desires of your heart.

> "If you remain in me and my words remain in you, ask whatever you wish, and it will be done for you."
> —JOHN 15:7 (NIV)

As you write the Word of God on the tablets of your heart, you are filling your heart with an abundance of God's Word. When your heart is full and you speak the Word, things will happen. You have the authority to use His Word.

When something is full, it will run over; it will overflow. That is what happens when you are full of the Word of God. If you are overflowing, the excess will flow onto others and they will be changed. When you allow Jesus to fill your heart today, you can be assured of your success tomorrow. Ask Jesus to bless your day; expect and believe you are blessed with victory, abundance, and protection.

Have a
JESUS
Filled Day

A DAY
FILLED WITH
ABUNDANCE

DAILY CONFESSION

Thank You, Lord, that I have life in abundance. Today, I have life to the fullest. I have life that is overflowing from the promises of Your Word. I receive the righteousness, peace, and joy that comes from a relationship with You, my Lord. As I live for You each day, I believe that I receive the success You have planned for my life.

Today, *I have A Day Filled with Abundance!*

CHAPTER TWELVE

A DAY
FILLED WITH
PROTECTION

"If you say, "The Lord is my refuge," and you
make the Most High your dwelling, no harm will
overtake you, no disaster will come near your
tent. For he will command his angels concerning
you to guard you in all your ways"
—PSALM 91:9-11 (NIV)

Moses found protection in Almighty God.
Moses decided that he was not going anywhere if
the Lord did not go
with him (Exodus
33:14). You should
feel the same way.
You need the pres-
ence of the Lord to
go with you (Exodus
33:15-18). If you do

"The Lord replied, 'My Presence will go with you, and I
will give you rest."
—EXODUS 33:14 (NIV)

not have His presence, then you should not want to go anywhere.

> "Whoever dwells in the shelter of the Most High will rest in the shadow of the Almighty."
> —PSALM 91:1 (NIV)

Moses is an example of how to follow God and experience His very presence. In both the Old and New Testaments, *A Day Filled with Protection* was a matter of dwelling and abiding in the Lord. It is in the presence of God that you are assured of receiving His promise of safety. No harm or disaster can overtake you. Then and now, we are all promised that He will send His angels to guard us. What an awesome God we serve, who personally protects the ones He loves.

> "The Lord is my light and my salvation – whom shall I fear?"
> —PSALM 27:1 (NIV)

Psalm 91 invites you to dwell in God's presence. You will find rest and protection in the very shadow of His presence. He covers you. Psalm 91 is full of promises for the believer who will dwell in that place of protection. When the Lord is the main focus in your life, there is no reason to be afraid. There is no fear when you have the light of the Lord in your life.

When you walk with Him, you will not stumble in the darkness. There is protection. When trials and temptations come, you will not fall because you have the promise of His presence to guide and shelter you. If you draw close to God, through His Word, prayer, praise, and worship, He promises to draw near to you. You can expect His protection, according to His Word.

PROTECTION FOR THE JESUS FILLED BE-LIEVER

Psalm 91:7 proclaims, "A thousand shall fall at thy side, and ten thousand at thy right hand; but it shall not come nigh thee." That verse tells you that He gives you protection. That protection is not earned. It costs you nothing. It is given to you because Jesus defeated death, hell, and the grave. All you have to do is believe and receive it. Through His Word, He gives us His promise of protection.

> "A thousand may fall at your side, ten thousand at your right hand, but it will not come near you."
> —PSALM 91:7 (NIV)

The Scriptures say that no weapon formed against you shall prosper (Isaiah 54:17). Weapons will be formed, but they will not prosper against you. It could be a weapon of sickness, disease, a lawsuit, or the loss of employment. No matter the weapon, when you are established in His covenant, you will overcome every obstacle. That is the heritage of the servants of the Lord.

If you are having a Jesus Filled Day, the eyes of the Lord are upon you. His ears are open to your cry because you are the reason Christ Jesus came to earth. He came to purchase your redemption.

Satan wants to steal your joy, your blessings, your health, and destroy your relationship with Christ. It is important to understand and believe, despite a rocky road and some detours or potholes along the way, that when you stay on the path, He will carry you safely to your expected destination.

> "No weapon forged against you will prevail . . ."
> —ISAIAH 54:17 (NIV)

DIVINE PROTECTION

Years ago, we took several members of our family with us to Israel. We flew from Houston to New York to catch a connecting flight. There were serious weather problems that delayed our flight. When we were finally allowed to take off, the plane was shaking as it tried to climb in altitude. We were being tossed and turned like a boat on a stormy sea. The devil started talking to us during that time about the possibility of something tragic happening to our family on board. What if we had made a mistake by bringing them along?

We began to pray and take authority over all negative thoughts from the enemy. We knew in our inner most being that God would answer our prayers, and He was still in control of the situation. We were confident that we would get to our destination by His grace because we knew that we had heard from God to bring our family with us.

The closer we got to New York, the worse the turbulence became. It was one of the most alarming events any of us had ever experienced. As we neared the airport, we were told that it had been closed. The weather was so bad we could not land. The pilot came on the intercom to let us know we were being diverted to another airport. Our connecting flight was in New York City. Another airport meant we were headed away from our connecting flight and the other group with whom we would be traveling. The pilot turned the plane towards a second airport.

In a little while, the pilot came back on the intercom to tell us the second airport was also closed, and he would have to find another place to land. The weather grew worse, as did the accompanying turbulence. As we headed toward a third airport, the voice of the pilot came over the intercom again, but this time he added something we were not expecting to hear. He told us the third airport was also closing, but would allow us to land because we were running out of fuel.

His words tried to open a way for fear to come in, but we did not allow it. We kept praying, knowing that the Lord was with us. He had *filled our day with protection* even though our day did not feel like it. In fact, our day, at that time, gave no indication that He was on the scene, or involved in our situation. It did not look like we were going to get off the plane alive. Even if we did, we were farther away from our destination.

In the natural, it seemed like we would not make the connecting flight. Finally, we were allowed to land, but we had to stay on the runway and could not taxi to the gate for a very long time. The pilot told us when we were landing that we would refuel and continue to our original airport as he had been notified it was reopened. When the weather was safe enough for us to taxi to the gate, the pilot then informed us he had changed his mind and was canceling that flight and parking the plane. We would need to make our own arrangements to continue our travel plans. After meeting with airport management, another plane and pilot were obtained and flew us to the first airport. Our family was able to meet with the rest of the group, and we were soon on our way to Israel.

When you are having *A Day Filled with Protection,* God's presence will go with you, no matter the country, state, or town in which you find yourself. Again we look to the Scriptures for the promises and reasons for which God is working in us, for us, and with us. He has a purpose! He pledged in Jeremiah 29:11 (NIV), "'For I know the plans I have for you,' declares the LORD, 'plans to prosper you and not to harm you, plans to give you hope and a future.'"

Have a
JESUS
Filled Day

A DAY
FILLED WITH
PROTECTION

DAILY CONFESSION

Thank You, Lord, that You have promised to protect me from all harm and danger. You are my stronghold and my shelter. You are my rock and source of strength. As I draw near to You, You draw near to me, according to Your Word. Thank You, Lord, that Your plans are to prosper me; giving me hope and a future.

Today, *I have A Day Filled with Protection!*

CHAPTER THIRTEEN

THE JESUS
FILLED DAY
DECISION

"This is the day the Lord hath made;
we will rejoice and be glad in it."
—PSALM 118:24

The Bible is very clear that the name of Jesus is above every name (Philippians 2:9). The name of Jesus is above sickness, poverty, lack, defeat, rejection, depression, low self-esteem, anger, loneliness, bitterness, addictions, self-centeredness, unforgiveness, resentment, hate, envy, pride, impatience, unfaithfulness, strife, grief, hopelessness, lack of faith, and everything else that keeps you bound. When you purpose in your heart to let Him fill your day, life is not so challenging.

When you let the name that is above every name, *Jesus,* fill your mind and emotions on a continual basis, you can have joy unspeakable and be full of glory (1 Peter 1:8). When you say, I am having a Jesus Filled Day, you are saying that Jesus is above everything else in your life. God loves you too much to leave you the way you are. What is it in your life that is keeping you from pursuing the Lord with all your heart? What person, activity, or material possession is in your way? You need to ask the Holy Spirit to examine your heart and help you overcome it. David asked that of the Lord in Psalm 139. He petitioned God, saying, "Search me, O God, and know my heart: Try me, and know my thoughts" (v. 23).

Jesus loves you and accepts you just the way you are. You can't earn His love. He is waiting for you to come to Him. When you come to Jesus, He begins to change your life. Every day that you fill with Jesus is a day where you are transformed into His image. Because Jesus loves you enough to accept you the way that you are, He wants to change you to become more like Him. The apostle Paul understood that when he told the Romans: ". . . He also predestined to be conformed to the image of His Son, that He might be the firstborn among many brethren," (Romans 8:29 NASB). God has already made the way possible to receive Jesus into your life forever and to enjoy an abundant, victorious life every day!

IT ALL STARTS WITH TODAY

Each day you will need to do what it takes to get the desired results of a Jesus Filled Day. You will have to make it a lifestyle and follow the plan of God. If you only decide to have a casual, infrequent relationship with Jesus, He won't have the opportunity to develop enough foundation to leave a significant impact on your life. Imagine going to the gym to lift weights. The guys who walk around in "muscle t-shirts" are usually the ones that are there five, or more, days a week. They sweat. They work hard. They take it very seriously and see the results. However, if they only go to the gym sporadically, choosing not to lift weights with a determined consistency, their bodies will not show significant change. In the same way, having a Jesus Filled Day is a decision that requires daily determination. In your life, you will see results as described in God's Word and this book, and others will see them as well.

You need to make a decision. Each day starts with you. No one will force you to fill your day with Jesus. The ball is in your court. The decision is on your shoulders. Jesus not only wants to fill up your day, but the rest of your life. Are you going to allow Jesus to fill up your day? Are you going to allow Him to be what you need Him to be? God will give you the strength only after you make the decision. God is looking for people who genuinely want to have a Jesus Filled Day. The Lord is looking for people who are excited about Him and want to serve Him. He is looking for people who will be separate; people not conformed to the world and who will replace worldly things with godly things.

He is looking for people who will believe exactly what He has said. He will keep His promises and fill every part of your life. Have you ever seen someone whose day was full of God? Have you ever seen someone so full of God's presence that you could sense the glory of God on them? When they enter a room, they change the atmosphere. It is God's desire for everyone to live a victorious, Jesus Filled Life, every day, moment by moment. Jesus is waiting for you to be that person whose life He can fill daily with His blessings, peace, abundance, protection, and so much more.

AN ETERNITY FILLED WITH JESUS

BEGINS WITH

PRAYER

"For God so loved the world, that he gave
his only begotten Son, that whosoever believeth
in him should not perish, but have
everlasting life. For God sent not his Son
into the world to condemn the world;
but that the world through him might be saved."
—JOHN 3:16-17

Have you ever tried to tune your radio to a certain station, but all you could hear was static, or
a weak signal? Eventually, you became so aggra-

vated that you turned it off because you could not get the station adjusted. Is that the way you have been with God? Have you ever felt that you were not getting through to Him? For example, your prayers may not have been answered as you expected, so you were becoming frustrated and aggravated with God.

The fault is not with God. He always wants to hear from you. He is always tuned in. God is looking for people who will seek His way of fine tuning themselves by humbling themselves before Him and committing all of their ways to His plan. People who desire peace with God and to know Him personally need to be tuned in, or connected, to God. You can open your heart and ask God to save you. Tell God you want to be accepted by Him and forgiven for your mistakes and sins. That is true humility and repentance. You are making a commitment to know Him as He has revealed Himself in His Son, Jesus. He is waiting for you to ask Him for help and to depend upon Him by faith in His Word.

Today, most people do not like the word "commitment." We all live in a world where we want to do things our way on our own time. If we don't want to go to church, we don't. If we don't want to pray, we don't. If we don't want to read the Bible, we don't. However, we all understand the commitment necessary to bring home a paycheck. If we decide that we don't feel like going to work, we will eventually lose our job. We also understand the commitment to keep our body strengthened through daily meals. If we don't eat, we lose strength and, in extreme circumstances, can even become sick due to malnutrition. In the same way we are committed to our job or to providing strength for our body through food, it is important for everyone to make a commitment to the work of God; to attend church faithfully, to read the Bible, and to pray every day.

It is so important that you don't let another moment pass without asking Jesus to be your Savior and begin an intimate relationship with Him through prayer, worship, and reading God's Word. You can't imagine how your life will be transformed when you are in close communion with Jesus Christ.

JESUS IS YOUR SAVIOR

"For God so loved the world that He gave His only begotten Son, that whoever believes in Him should not perish but have everlasting life." —John 3:16 (NIV)

"For the Son of Man has come to seek and to save that which was lost." —Luke 19:10 (NASB)

"But God demonstrates His own love for us in this: While we were still sinners, Christ died for us." —Romans 5:8 (NIV)

"That if you confess with thy mouth the Lord Jesus, and shalt believe in thine heart that God hath raised him from the dead, thou shalt be saved. For with the heart man believeth unto righteousness; and with the mouth confession is made unto salvation." —Romans 10:9-10

To accept Jesus Christ as your personal Lord and Savior, pray the following prayer.

Dear Heavenly Father, I come to You in the name of Jesus. I am sorry for my sins and the life I have lived. I believe Jesus died on the cross for my sins. I ask You to forgive me and cleanse me with the blood of Jesus for all the sins and unrighteousness in my life. You said in Your Holy Word that if I confess and believe in my heart that God raised Jesus from the dead, I will be saved. Right now, I confess Jesus Christ as Lord over my life and receive Him as my own personal Savior. According to Your Word, I am now saved by God's grace! Amen.

If you prayed that prayer, you are now a new person.

A NEW CREATION THROUGH JESUS CHRIST

"Therefore, if anyone be in Christ, he is a new creature; old things are passed away; behold, all things are become new." —2 Corinthians 5:17

"Verily, verily, I say unto you, He that believeth on me hath everlasting life." — John 6:47.

PRAYER OF COMMITMENT

As you have read, there is so much more to living the Christian life than just simple routines, often lacking *Jesus' daily presence*. God has much greater plans for your life! We invite you to pray the following prayer, dedicating your life to Jesus in every way; allowing Him to be part of everything you do, allowing you to *Have a Jesus Filled Day.*

Jesus, thank You for loving me. Thank You for dying for all of my sins, all my mistakes, and all the times I have missed the mark. Thank You for paying a price I could never pay. I am so grateful that You came to earth to make a way for me to be able to live with a sense of Your presence each day.

I recognize that I need You in my life. Today, I know that I want You to be a part of everything to do with my life: my words, my actions, my thoughts, and everything I am. I commit to allowing You to be the Lord of my life. You are in charge. I desire You to be the director of my life. I promise to do my very best to grow in my understanding of You. I also pledge to change the way I view each day.

No longer do I want to live for myself and my agenda. I don't want to know about You or only think of You on Sundays. I want every day to be filled with a sense of Your presence in my life. *I want every day, from this point forward, to be a Jesus Filled Day! Amen.*

If you have prayed either of those prayers, committing your life entirely to Jesus, we would like to hear from you. Please write to us at: P.O. Box 34, Houston, TX 77001. God bless you and may all your days be Jesus Filled!

Have a
JESUS
Filled Day

A DAY
FILLED WITH
COMMITMENT

DAILY CONFESSION

Today, Lord, I will be in tune with You. I am committed to You and Your ways. I desire Your will for my life. Today, I will serve You with all of my heart, all of my mind, all of my soul, and all of my strength.

Today, *I have A Day Filled with Commitment!*

APPENDIX

CONFESSIONS
FOR A
JESUS
FILLED DAY

We believe in the power of confessing the Word of God over our lives. In Matthew 21:21-22, Jesus said these words: ". . . if you have faith, and doubt not . . . if ye shall say to this mountain, Be thou removed and be thou cast into the sea; it shall be done. And all things whatever ye ask in prayer, believing, ye shall receive." What powerful verses of Scripture. If people believe and speak according to the Word of God, those verses confirm that they will have whatever they say. There is power in your words when they are spoken from the Word of God! Below are confessions that we encourage you to speak over your life on a daily basis. They are based on each chapter of this book. As you make these confessions, believe that you receive what you say and you will have it!

A DAY FILLED WITH JESUS

Thank You, Lord, that as I desire to meet with You today, You desire to meet me in return. Thank You that I recognize my need for You. I don't need anyone or anything other than You. As I seek You, I will find You, according to Your Word.

Today, *I have A Day Filled with Jesus!*

A DAY FILLED WITH LIFE

Thank You, Lord, that there is power in Your Word. Thank You that as I speak Your Word, in faith, I am able to have confidence that You will answer every prayer that I pray. Thank You that I am delivered from all death and destruction. Thank You that my life has been redeemed from the pit of death and despair. I believe that as I confess Your Word, I receive everything that I pray, in the name of Jesus.

Today, *I have A Day Filled with Life!*

A DAY FILLED WITH BLESSINGS

Thank You, Lord, that I am blessed in every way. I am the head and not the tail; above and not beneath. Thank You for every blessing You have brought to my life. I do not take any of them for granted but am grateful that You love me and cause me to be blessed because I love You. I do not operate in fear. I do not operate under stress, but I am open to receive every good and perfect gift that You have for me.

Today, *I have A Day Filled with Blessings!*

A DAY FILLED WITH VICTORY

Thank You, Lord, that I live all of my days filled with victory. Thank You that I am able to overcome every storm that comes my way, as I trust in You. I am so glad that You, oh God, are bigger than any problem that I will ever face. Thank You that I don't have to deal with my struggles on my own. I place them in Your hands, giving You permission to handle every situation. Thank You Lord, that as I keep pressing forward in the midst of every trial, that I speak Your Word and see victory in every area of my life.

Today, *I have A Day Filled with Victory!*

A DAY FILLED WITH MIRACLES

Thank You, Lord, for being the same yesterday, today, and forever. The same miracles that You displayed 2,000 years ago are the same miracles that You want to display in my life today. No matter what the circumstance in my life demands, You are a miracle-working Savior. With You, all things are possible.

Today, *I have A Day Filled with Miracles!*

A DAY FILLED WITH FAVOR

Thank You, Lord, that I walk in Your favor. You are a great God and have wonderful plans for my life. I trust You with all of my heart and do not lean on my own understanding. I know You have my best interest in Your heart. I expect doors to open and people to work on my behalf, according to the plans You have for my life. Everything works for the good in my life because I love You and am called according to Your purpose.

Today, *I have A Day Filled with Favor!*

A DAY FILLED WITH SATISFACTION

Thank You, Lord, that Your desire is to satisfy me. I do not seek instant gratification but allow You to satisfy every need that I have. I do not push You out of any area of my life. Instead, I seek to have an intimate friendship and relationship with You, allowing me to be satisfied with Your goodness.

Today, *I have A Day Filled with Satisfaction!*

A DAY FILLED with PEACE

Thank You, Lord, that I have the ability to cast every burden, every concern, every worry, and every fear on Your shoulders. In return, You give me peace that passes my understanding. Trials and tests may come, but I choose to remain anchored in You, oh Lord. You hold me secure as I find my peace in You.

Today, *I have A Day Filled with Peace!*

A DAY FILLED with GUIDANCE

Thank You, Lord, that my steps are ordered by You. I don't place my trust in money, a man, or any other type of security. I rely completely on You. You are trustworthy, and I have faith in You and Your Word. Lord, You are my strength, my refuge, my strong tower, my peace, my healer, and my fortress. Thank You, Lord, that You are my guide. You lead, guide, and direct every step I take.

Today, I have *A Day Filled with Guidance!*

A DAY FILLED with VISION

Today, Lord, I see through the eyes of faith. I believe the impossible is possible through You. No matter what the signs around are telling me, I hold to the promises of Your Word. I believe Your Word is truth that is above the opinions of man and the circumstances I observe. I choose to have vision. I choose to see myself and the condition of my life the way that You reveal it to me.

Today, *I have A Day Filled with Vision!*

A DAY FILLED WITH ABUNDANCE

Thank You, Lord, that I have life in abundance. Today, I have life to the fullest. I have life that is overflowing from the promises of Your Word. I receive the righteousness, peace, and joy that comes from a relationship with You, my Lord. As I live for You each day, I believe that I receive the success You have planned for my life.

Today, I have *A Day Filled with Abundance!*

A DAY FILLED WITH PROTECTION

Thank You, Lord, that You have promised to protect me from all harm and danger. You are my stronghold and my shelter. You are my rock and source of strength. As I draw near to You, You draw near to me, according to Your Word. Thank You, Lord, that Your plans are to prosper me; giving me hope and a future.

Today, I have *A Day Filled with Protection!*

A DAY FILLED WITH COMMITMENT

Today, Lord, I will be in tune with You. I am committed to You and Your ways. I desire Your will for my life. Today, I will serve You with all of my heart, all of my mind, all of my soul, and all of my strength.

Today, I have *A Day Filled with Commitment!*

> EACH TIME THE SUN RISES,
> KNOW THAT IT IS HIS DESIRE
> FOR YOU TO "HAVE A JESUS
> FILLED DAY!"

ABOUT THE AUTHOR

Roy Chapman is a dynamic speaker in the Christian community. Healing evangelists A. A. Allen, Jack Coe, as well as other men and women of God have impacted his life. As a result, the power of the Holy Spirit in his ministry has helped many people experience amazing miracles.

Roy founded Chosen Ministries, Inc., an international outreach ministry. He is also the pastor of Worship Tabernacle, a non-denominational church in Humble, Texas.

Roy has made guest appearances on the local Trinity Broadcasting Network and Daystar Television Network, as well as radio talk shows. Roy has been a speaker for the local TBN prayer partner services and a guest speaker at the Christmas Banquet. He was also the host of *Rejoice in the Lord*, a Christian talk show which aired on Channel 22 known as *Keep Looking to Jesus*. Now, the program airs on ChosenNetwork.TV Roku channel and the Internet.

To order additional copies of this book as well as other products visit our website at
www.WorshipTabernacle.tv

Or by writing or faxing:
Have a Jesus Filled Day Corporation™
P.O. Box 34
Houston, Texas 77001
(281) 399-3840 fax
Thank you for your support!

NOTES

NOTES

NOTES

NOTES

www.ingramcontent.com/pod-product-compliance
Lightning Source LLC
LaVergne TN
LVHW021508080426
835509LV00018B/2442

9780998748672